WeeSing® & 123

Wee Sing® & Learn
123

by Pamela Conn Beall and Susan Hagen Nipp
illustrated by Yudthana Pongmee

PRICE STERN SLOAN

1 one

1 whale

Can you count one of anything else?

2 two

2 dolphins

Can you count two of anything else?

3 three

3 sea otters

Can you count three of anything else?

4 four

4 squids

Can you count four of anything else?

5 five

5 sea stars

Can you count five of anything else?

6 six

6 turtles

Can you count six of anything else?

7 seven

7 lobsters

Can you count seven of anything else?

8 eight

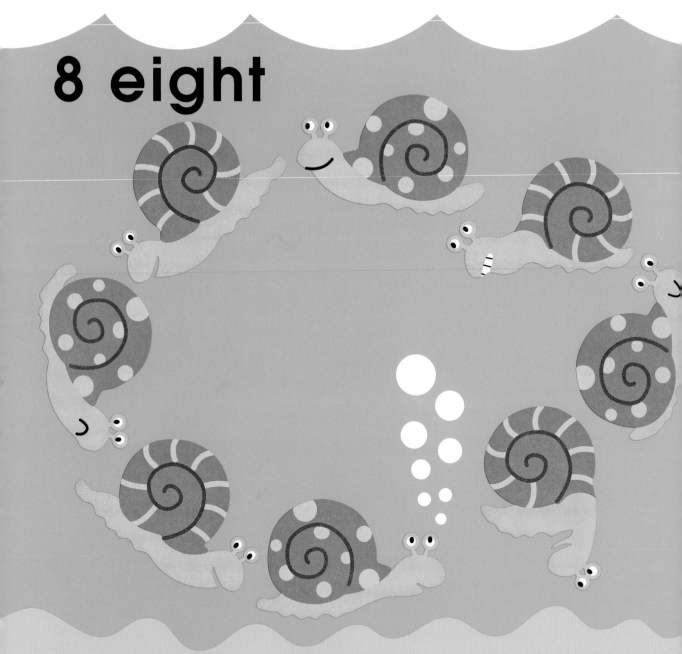

8 sea snails

Can you count eight of anything else?

9 nine

9 puffer fish

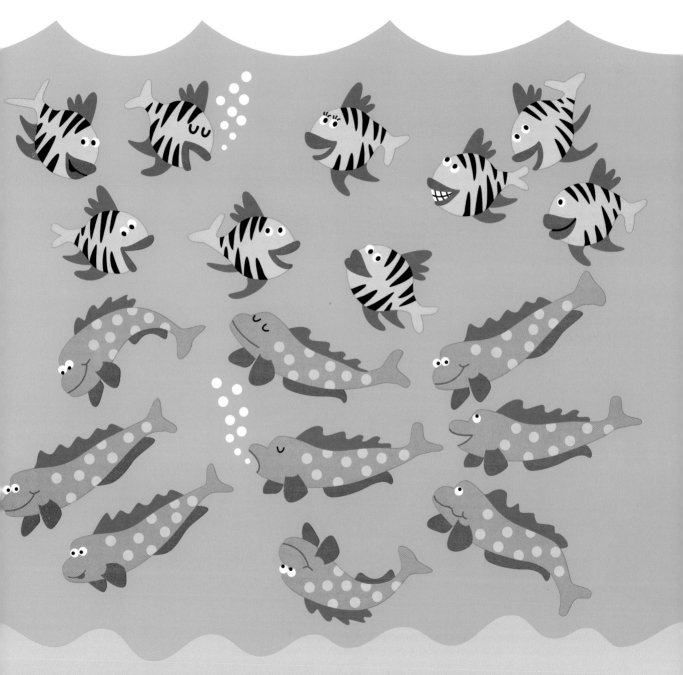

Can you count nine of anything else?

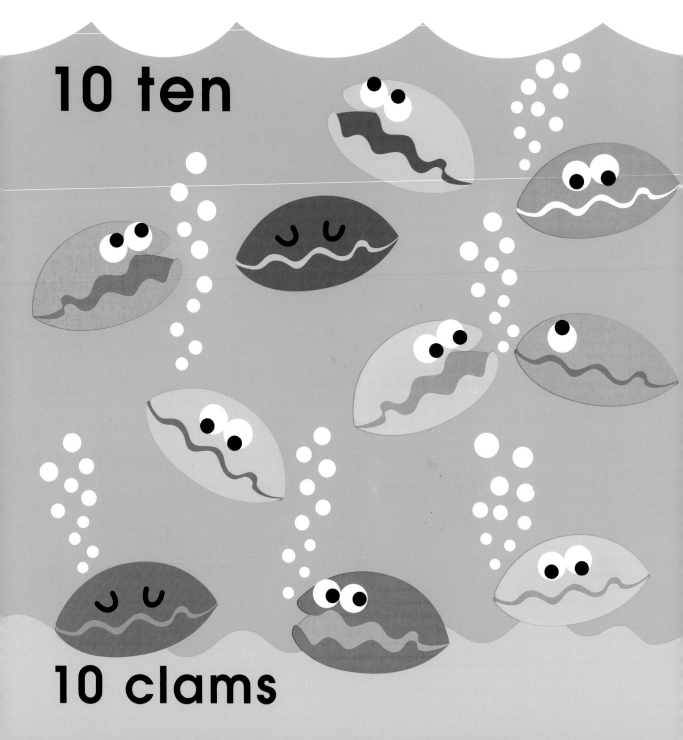

10 ten

10 clams

Can you count ten of anything else?

11 eleven

11 seahorses

Can you count eleven of anything else?

12 twelve

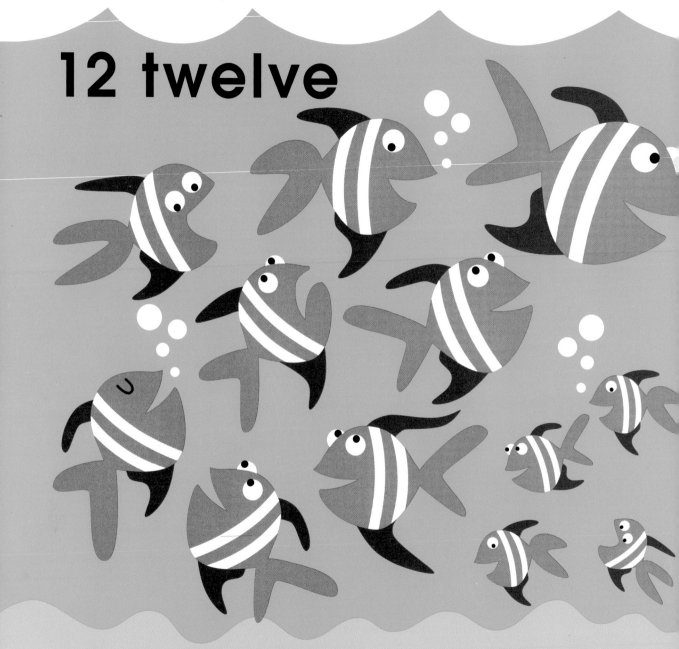

12 angelfish

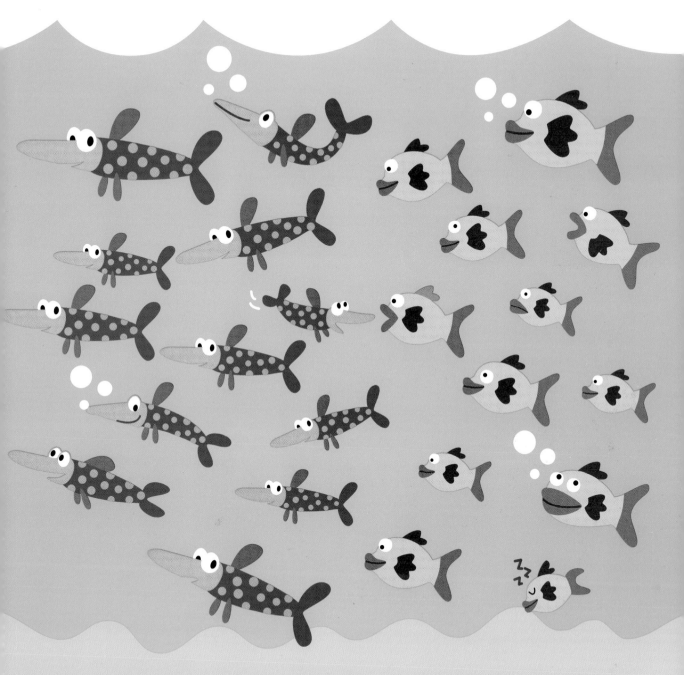

Can you count twelve of anything else?

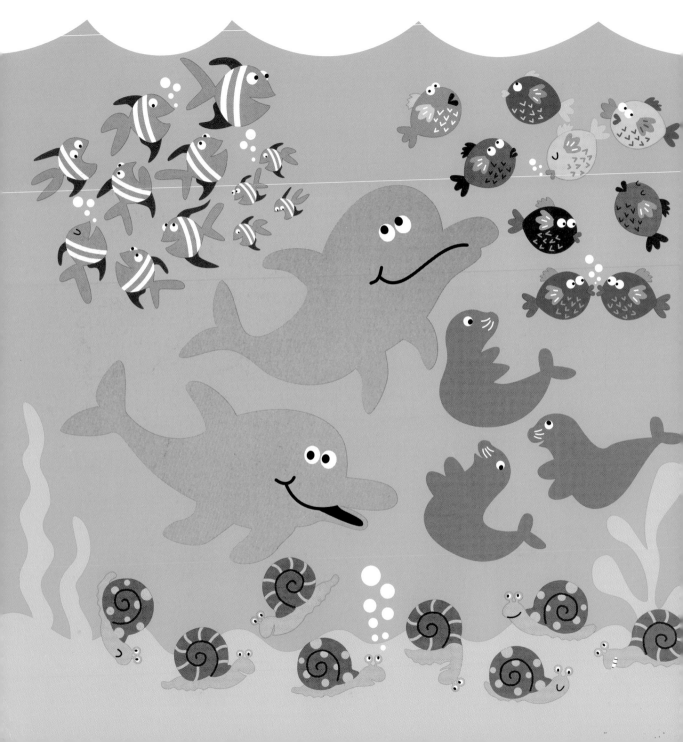

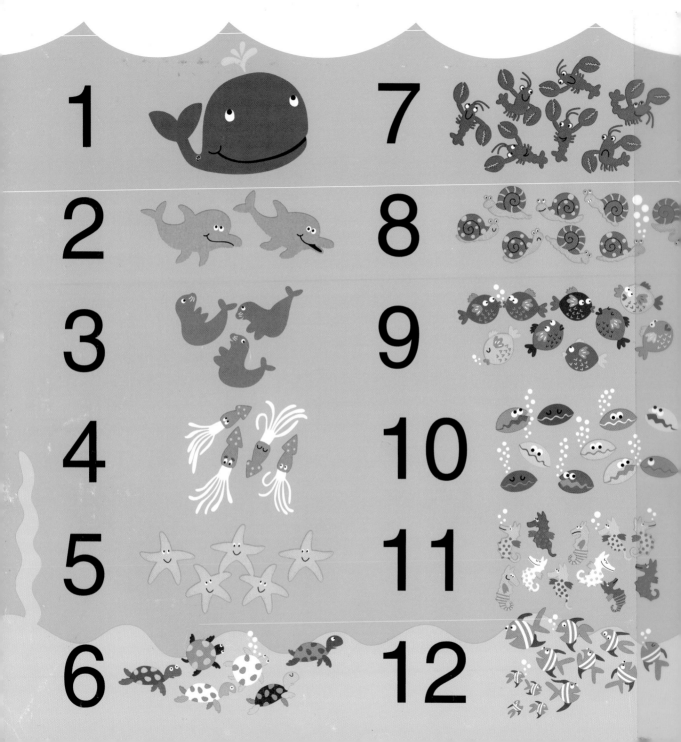